SWAMI VIVEKANANDA
IN SAN FRANCISCO

SWAMI ASHOKANANDA

VEDANTA SOCIETY OF NORTHERN CALIFORNIA
SAN FRANCISCO, CALIFORNIA
1990

ISBN 0-9612388-2-8

Swami Vivekananda in San Francisco *is a combination of three lectures of that title delivered extemporaneously at the Vedanta Society of Northern California in San Francisco by Swami Ashokananda. The first two lectures were given on January 7, 1946, and February 16, 1949, at the Old Temple and were taken down in shorthand. The third was delivered on July 4, 1965, at the New Temple and recorded on tape. In combining the transcripts of these three lectures some omissions have necessarily been made, but the essential points of each lecture have been retained.*

In this edition extracts from six of the lectures that Swami Vivekananda delivered in San Francisco have been added.

CONTENTS

SWAMI VIVEKANANDA
IN SAN FRANCISCO

SWAMI VIVEKANANDA
IN SAN FRANCISCO

1

Today we are celebrating the birthday of Swami Vivekananda, and I have thought that since this Vedanta Society was founded by him, it would be fitting that we give a little attention to what he did and said in San Francisco. Certainly the Swami's words and teachings in this city should have a particular significance for those of us who live here, especially those who come to this center and are interested in spiritual development. But the canvas, I admit, is rather narrow, and it would not be desirable this morning to deal exclusively with the details of his stay in this one place. Probably there are some among you who know very little about him, and thus, though the details of his visit in San Francisco are very impressive, they would not in themselves convey to you any particular meaning. I shall also try to give you, therefore, a general idea of the Swami and his life.

He was a tremendously great man, one of the world's very few messengers of light. You probably feel I am saying this from the Oriental habit of exaggeration. Nothing of the kind! I did not see Swami Vivekananda in the flesh, but I have lived with many people who knew him intimately—his great brother disciples, who had known him from boyhood, and his own disciples, some of whom had met him in the very early years of his mission. So it was possible for me to receive firsthand impressions from these direct associates, all of whom said that no language was adequate to express his greatness.

How can I tell you what he was? He was a man about whom you could form no idea unless you actually saw him. You could not even imagine that a human being could be so great, so wonderful, so full of power, wisdom, and all kinds of perfections. Even his Master, Sri Ramakrishna, who is recognized in India by millions and millions of Hindus as an embodiment of Divinity of the same caliber as Buddha and Christ, could come to no end in describing his greatness. This was sometimes very embarrassing to Swami Vivekananda, because in his presence the Master would compare him, a boy barely out of his teens, with the spiritually great religious leaders of the time and declare him superior to them. The Swami would conclude that his Master was a little touched in the head—all right on certain points but just obsessed on this one point. Yet all that Sri Ramakrishna said about him proved later to be true.

Sri Ramakrishna had seen Swami Vivekananda in a vision long before he met him. Many times he said that he had gone to a transcendental realm and brought this great soul to the earth for the good of mankind. Thus when the Swami first came to visit Sri Ramakrishna at the Dakshineswar Temple, the Master was ready for him and from the beginning treated him with the utmost respect. He stood before his prospective disciple with folded hands in the attitude of worship and adoration and said to him, "Lord, why have you taken so long to come? I know you are born on earth to remove the misery of mankind. I have been waiting so long for you!" He would never allow this disciple to render him any of the services usually done by a pupil for his teacher, so great was his respect for him.

But if the Swami could not understand at first why Sri Ramakrishna held him in such high regard, he later came to know of the importance of his own existence and his own mission. As I have pointed out to you many times before, in answer to a question in Brooklyn he said, "I have a message for the West as Buddha had a message for the East."[1] He knew his power and the strength of his message and the effectiveness of it. He did not have the slightest doubt. He used to claim that he could see clearly the next three or four hundred years spread before his eyes. Many have thought he spoke like this just out of enthusiasm, and others that he was being overemphatic in accordance with his vigorous mind. But I have heard it said again and again by his brother monks, and it was also said by his Master, that Swami Vivekananda was one of the most truthful of men. He never said anything just for effect; he did not have to.

I should mention here, for it has bearing on my main topic, that the Swami was not only great among the spiritually great, he was also unique. Indeed Sri Ramakrishna said that such a man had not been born before and would not be born again. Many who read his books and lectures think his teachings are just repetitions of the old truths. Even among his dedicated followers some are content to say he taught the Advaita (monistic Vedanta) as taught by Shankara, or that he taught the same things his Master taught, or that he harmonized all the different aspects of the spiritual ideal—such as knowledge, devotion, and action—but they find nothing original or new about his message. Of course, they admit there is a certain newness: just as new life springs from old bulbs when you plant them in the garden, so new life can spring from old religious truths. It is recognized that there is that kind of newness in the Swami's message. But not many realize that his teachings were completely different even in the enunciation of the recognized spiritual paths. In propounding all the truths that should be put before people—the nature of religion, the definition of spiritual ideals, the ways and means by which a man can become free and realize his lost divinity—in all these things he was unique. Don't say, "No, there are only traces of originality here and there." If you think I am exaggerating or making too much of it, I would request you to study the life of Swami Vivekananda and his teachings with thoughtfulness. He was so great that if you spent your whole life trying to grasp him not many of you would succeed to the extent that you could say with assurance, "I know who you are." I myself do not claim to have done so, but I have given many years of thought to Swami Vivekananda as a person and to the study of his ideas, and I do claim this much: I am always seeing new things in his personality and his teachings that require my further study. More and more I find things still beyond my intellect to grasp; more and more new depths of thought are revealed. I make this observation here because I have found that while the Swami was staying in California, especially in San Francisco, he propounded certain ideas to which I have not seen him give so bold and insistent a voice in any other place. Probably San Francisco is a special city; San Franciscans certainly always think so. But I really do think this city is especially blessed in being the locale where Swami Vivekananda taught things that he did not teach with the same strength, openness, and decisiveness anywhere else.

The Swami was in the Bay Region from the last week of February to the end of May 1900. For about three weeks in April he lived in an old mansion belonging to the Home of Truth in Alameda (now there is a hotel on the site); another two weeks he spent in Marin County, camping under the redwoods; but most of the time—nine weeks in all—he lived in San Francisco. He walked the streets of this city, and the whole city has become sanctified. He was in the halls and eating places and stores; he went to your Golden Gate Park; he was fond of going to Chinatown; he crossed the Bay many times on your ferryboats, which unfortunately are no longer there. He lectured and gave classes in several places; he spoke in the First Unitarian Church of Oakland, and in Alameda he spoke in a public hall and also in the Home of Truth; all these places became holy places because of his having been there and having taught in them.

Indeed as I stand before you to talk about how he came to this city and lived here, what he said and what he did, I can only think, as a parallel, of the traditions that have grown around the great ones like Christ. For example, if you are a devout Christian and go to Jerusalem, you will recognize certain places there and say, this is where the Christ walked, this is the gate by which he entered the city, this is where he performed a miracle. That little bit of earth you will look upon not as just a geographical point but as something precious beyond human calculation. Now suppose by some magic you suddenly began to think that this city of San Francisco had been blessed and consecrated by the footsteps of the Lord Jesus or even by those of Saint Paul or Saint Peter: What would you think of your city? What would you think of those spots where such a person preached or walked or took his meal? I have not the least doubt, although I know that in so saying I shall appear to you more a fanatic than a reasonable man, that those places in San Francisco where Swami Vivekananda lived will become places to visit, holy places in which to sit and meditate with the faith and hope that there one will be able to come more easily into contact with the divine presence.

Remember this: here in the Bay Area the Swami had constant God-vision; here he saw God shining in everyone. Consider the blessedness of having one person living among us who even *once* in his life had this vision; such are not found in abundance. We hear of saints who had a single distant glimpse—that was all they had. But here was a man who day and night, without any effort, remained in a transcendent state and saw God everywhere.

2

Let me give a brief outline of the Swami's life. He was born on January 12, 1863; he passed away on July 4, 1902. But though he lived only a little more than thirty-nine years, during those years he accomplished a tremendous amount. He was the eldest son of an aristocratic family of Calcutta. It is said that his mother, as is customary in India, regularly worshiped Shiva before she conceived him. Also a relative of hers who lived in Banaras went every day to the temple of Vireswara

Shiva, a small but beautiful temple, and there on her behalf offered worship. So when the child was born he was given the name Vireswara. That name, however, was rarely used; he became known, rather, as Narendra, "the king of men." He was a turbulent child, and his mother would often become annoyed at him and say, "I prayed to Shiva to give me a good son, and He has sent me one of His demons." When he was especially turbulent, she would pour a jug of cold water over his head and take the name of Shiva. That was how she kept him under control. He would just quiet down. He used to say in later years, "The moment my mother would mention the name of Shiva, I would think, this time I must be good."

When he reached his teens, the desire to realize God became very strong in him. It became almost an obsession with him to ask every religious teacher he met if he had actually seen God. Not a single person could say yes. In this way several years passed, until in 1881 when he was eighteen years old he came to know Sri Ramakrishna. At one time Sri Ramakrishna had worshiped as a priest in one of the chapels of the Dakshineswar Temple, a few miles north of Calcutta on the Ganges. Afterwards he became such a great knower of God it was no longer possible for him to do any formal worship; he just lived in a room in the temple precincts—a bare room with a cot. As he became known, people from all over India, though particularly from Calcutta, would come to see him. Many of them were well-known religious leaders. They used to sit entranced at his feet and observe him in the state of God-consciousness, giving God-realization to people by a look, a touch, or a word. Whoever came he would fill to the brim—not by giving lectures or private interviews. No such thing! If a man was ready, he would give him God-realization at once. If not, he gave him the power to go ahead. Literally, by one touch, one word he would change the course of a man's life. Further, the things he spoke were not just words, they were a part of his own being. He lived those things; when he spoke of the signs or the means of God-realization, he manifested them clearly. Thus it was that when Swami Vivekananda went to see the Master his quest was ended: Sri Ramakrishna told him yes, he had seen God and could teach him also to see God.

Sri Ramakrishna passed away in 1886, so that the Swami was with him less than five years. A good part of this time passed in a continual battle between the disciple and the Master. Master was great, disciple was great. The disciple refused to believe in the Master's spiritual experiences and visions. Though as time went on he saw the greatness of Sri Ramakrishna and loved him deeply, still he would not accept his realizations.

In those days, you see, Swami Vivekananda was exceedingly skeptical. The one predominant characteristic of modern thinking is skepticism. As a matter of fact, the whole structure of the knowledge of the modern age is more or less stimulated by skepticism. It is as senseless to say one should not use an automobile as to say, "Do not be a skeptic." But while Swami Vivekananda was a skeptic, he was not without exceedingly high ideals. There were certain things he felt he must do and observe. He was the purest of men. He never could do anything or tolerate anything that was impure or untrue; about that he could not make the slightest conces-

sion or compromise. There was also that hunger in his soul for something beyond the world of forms, the world of the senses. Without being told how to meditate, he used to meditate. In later times he would say, "If there is not a spiritual Reality, what is the good of this existence? And if there *is* such a Reality, then this life is not worth living—it is too demeaning, too low to be lived."[2] He used to feel like that; and his heart would yearn for something. He went about restless. When Sri Ramakrishna first saw him, he said "I could not believe a person like him could live in a worldly city like Calcutta. He is *dhyana siddha* (established in meditation)." "Established" means it was natural for him to be meditative. He saw that a good part of the Swami's mind was plunged in meditation all the time.

Sri Ramakrishna understood and approved his disciple's skepticism and used to say to him, "Do not accept anything on faith. Test me. Experience for yourself." Nevertheless within five years he converted the Swami. That was not a conversion by persuasion, where a greater mind bears down upon another mind and deals blow after blow, whether cushioned in kid gloves or dealt by a mailed fist; Sri Ramakrishna never believed in that kind of conversion. Rather, he brought out all the disciple's spiritual powers, all his latent ability for spiritual perception. Step by step the Master gave him an extraordinary training.

First, he made him a monist. Before the Swami went to Sri Ramakrishna he had been a member of a theistic society patterned after Unitarian Christianity, the Brahmo Samaj. Many parts of Hinduism entered into its doctrines, but it rejected many other parts. The Brahmos

condemned image worship: like the followers of Semitic religions, they thought it was idol worship, positively an obstruction, and therefore sinful; they believed in a Personal God, but without form; they believed in dualism; and they believed that souls were ignorant, helpless, small and that through devotion or prayer they attained salvation. The Swami often attended the meetings of the Samaj and was imbued with its ideas. Then he came to visit Sri Ramakrishna and found that Sri Ramakrishna went into the temple and worshiped the images! Worse, Sri Ramakrishna worshiped Kali, a form repulsive to the Swami; worse still, he used to speak of Her continually and have visions of Her.

If you see pictures of Kali, you will be terrified—dark complexion, loose hair, a garland of skulls about her neck, covered with blood—a terrible Goddess! But if you want to worship God through a symbol (and that is a valid practice), probably the symbol of Kali is the most abstruse, inclusive, and comprehensive of all divine symbols. There is no denying that God Himself cuts off many heads. God's hands are covered with blood; you cannot deny that. Many of you have come here thinking you will hear what you have already heard in Christian churches. Why should I repeat what you are accustomed to hear? The time has come when we should know everything we can about God. The time has come to enlarge our vision. You say God creates and maintains, but when it comes to destroying the world you think, "No, no. God had nothing to do with that!" If not, then He has nothing to do with creation either. The creative process is linked with the process of destruction. You cannot deny it. Who kills men? Who brings death, epidemics, famine? Who is

responsible for the horrible massacres which you call war? Who? He whose power runs this universe—the Creator, Maintainer and Destroyer. If you have to hold anybody responsible for death, it is God you will have to hold responsible, God who is the Cause of all causes. But when you think of destruction associated with God, you cannot look upon it in the same way as when you associate it with a man. The purpose of such a teaching is not to show that God is a vile person but to show that what you consider vile is not really vile. Even what you call evil is divine. We are afraid of certain things; we run away and call them evil; we do not want to associate these things with God. We like certain other things, and these things alone we associate with God. There is just stupidity and ignorance in such a way of thinking! If you have the eyes to see, you see that all is divine.

So Sri Ramakrishna worshiped this Goddess, and Swami Vivekananda was horrified. He said, "I won't accept it." Gradually, however, the Master took him away from the dualism taught by the Brahmo Samaj. First, as I said, he made him a monist. The essence of monism, in very bold words, is this: one says, "I am He. I am all the reality. If the truth is anywhere, that is myself. I am God, I am Brahman." It is a startling thing for a man to say, but that is what Sri Ramakrishna taught him. It was not just a verbal teaching; Swami Vivekananda actually experienced it.

Then Sri Ramakrishna gave him another training. After weaning him away from this crude dualism, after making him a nondualist, he made him a devotee of the Divine Mother. That is a long but very beautiful story. To make it brief, the Swami's family had become destitute after the sudden death of his father, and when he could not earn enough money to support them and pay their debts, in desperation he asked Sri Ramakrishna to pray to his Divine Mother for help. The Master told him he would have to pray to Her himself and said, "Go to the Kali temple tonight, prostrate before the Mother, and whatsoever you ask will be granted." As the Swami approached the temple he forgot his need and was filled with great devotion. All he could ask for were spiritual blessings. Three times he went but could ask for nothing material. Then Sri Ramakrishna, pleased that he could not pray for anything but God Himself, said, "All right, your family will never lack for coarse rice and coarse cloth"—the bare necessities.

Many of you will remember reading of this incident, but probably you do not know that later that night an extraordinary thing happened; the Swami had an actual vision of the Mother. She appeared before him and blessed him. She also extracted a promise from him—henceforth, until he had finished Her work, he would be Her slave. You see, the Mother of the Universe has another side: She also grants boons and takes care of us, and She wanted the Swami to become Her instrument for the good of mankind. And the Swami promised. On a rare occasion many years later he spoke of this vision to a Western disciple. "She made a slave of me," he said. "Those were the very words—'a slave of you.' And Ramakrishna Paramahamsa made me over to Her."[3] He was a dynamic personality and could not stand anything binding, limiting to the human spirit; yet he was as it were held down here.

Not long after the Divine Mother had extracted that

promise from Swami Vivekananda, Sri Ramakrishna's health failed. But before he passed away he called the Swami to his side, and all his spiritual powers, all his spiritual knowledge, all that he had, he transferred to this disciple. You may wonder how the Master could give his power and knowledge to anyone. But it can be done. You remember in the Christian tradition the laying on of hands by which Christ communicated power to the disciples? The great ones can do it. Swami Vivekananda once said in later years, "Just as I give you a flower and know I have given it, and you know you have received it, in the same way one can transfer spiritual power to another person." Transferring everything in this way to his disciple, Sri Ramakrishna then said, "With the help of this power you will do tremendous good to mankind." In our Order we always think that henceforth Sri Ramakrishna and the Mother of the Universe lived in Swami Vivekananda. He often used to say that they directed him and that his words and actions proceeded from them.

A few days before his passing Sri Ramakrishna said to Swamiji, "I leave all my boys in your charge. You train them." He was referring to those disciples who were to become the first members of the monastic order of Ramakrishna. After the Master died, Swami Vivekananda felt full responsibility for their welfare and undertook to give them proper training. Of course they were spiritually very great, but spirituality has to be directed. You may have spiritual power, but how you will direct it depends on your having a certain outlook. You could bring it to the service of man, or you could exhaust it within the confines of a shrine, doing ritualistic worship, as has happened in India. You see this in the proliferation of temples; the currents of spiritual power have flowed into these temples and become locked up there. Swami Vivekananda did not want that to happen to the spiritual power Sri Ramakrishna had generated.

Then as time went on he realized he had another responsibility, that he must take the message of the Master all over the world. He had wandered over the whole of India and mingled with all kinds of people; a deep feeling for the service of man had awakened within him, and he had become filled with tremendous compassion. So much so that on the eve of his departure to the West in May, 1893, he said, "I am willing to go to hell if thereby I can help one person."

It was in San Francisco that Swami Vivekananda told a woman disciple, "You know, I may have to be born again. You see, I have fallen in love with man." His Master himself said that he was the incarnation of Man. You won't understand that—unless I tell you that in India there is a legendary belief that in the very beginning of creation the Lord became incarnated in two divine forms and as long as this creation exists the two must remain. They are Nara (Man) and Narayana (God). Both exist simultaneously. It was in reference to this belief—if you think deeply you will find it has a profound philosophical basis—that Sri Ramakrishna said Swami Vivekananda was the incarnation of Man. And it is a fact that the Swami believed himself to be identified with all men, nor has there been another great spiritual teacher in the history of the world who so took into consideration all the various phases of human life. Almost all other teachers have been concerned only with man's *spiritual* welfare—a few slightly with other aspects. But Swami Vivekananda was interested in every aspect of man; his aim was that all men and women should be so developed that they could realize not only their spiritual nature, which is identical with Divinity, but also their potentialities and capacities, whether esthetic, philosophical, intellectual, or active. None of the ways mankind has expressed greatness should be scorned or neglected.

It was his conviction that religions have often brought ruin to people by stunting their growth. If you say, "I want only the flower that is growing on the topmost branch of the tree, and so I'll cut off all the other branches," you ruin the tree and don't even get a good flower on the top branch; whereas if you allow the tree to grow fully and naturally, every branch, including the top one, will blossom with wonderful flowers. Many religions say, "This is spiritual; this is worldly." When people cut off everything worldly in order to become spiritual, they forget that human nature is an organic whole and each part of that nature is dependent on the other parts. The art lies in knowing which part should be allowed to grow and what its relation is to the other parts. This is how our monks are trained. It is quite an art, and Swami Vivekananda wanted that art cultivated. I think in this respect he consciously did what other great teachers and guides have not done.

Whatever that might be, he began to feel that he had a certain mission to fulfill. Partly he felt it was a responsibility given to him by his Master, and partly, being a master himself, he himself felt there was something he should and must do for man. Under the impact of these motives he began to feel, toward the beginning of 1893, that he was ready. He saw a vision in which his Master pointed out that he should cross the water and go to the West. He did not take it seriously at first, but afterwards he had no doubt about it.

So he came to this country and in September of 1893 appeared on the platform of the Parliament of Religions in Chicago. That was how his work in the West began. At the Parliament he was an instantaneous success. Those who arranged the programs would schedule his talks for the end of a session, because they found the audiences would sit through hours and hours of tedious speeches just for the sake of hearing him, if only for fifteen minutes or so.

Afterwards he lectured in different towns and cities in the central and eastern states. Sometimes he would give fourteen lectures in a week—often tremendously long lectures, two and a half hours or more. He just couldn't stop; but he spoke fire. Further, he organized the work here. He felt there was a need for Vedanta in this country; so he first started a center in New York and then he published several books of his teachings. All the while he kept up a voluminous correspondence. It was, in fact, through his many letters from this country that he began to organize the work in India. He visited England in 1895 and again in 1896. After staying in London the second time for four or five months, he went back to India. That was at the end of 1896. By that time his health had practically broken down. The tremendous amount of work he did in this country! It could not but ruin his health.

Another thing that told on his body was that his mind rose and remained permanently so high that he could not easily bring it down. Just as people who have lived in high altitudes find it hard to return to the plains where the air is too thick, too dirty, too hot, similarly the mind sometimes rises so high and becomes so accustomed to the elevations of the soul that it cannot come down.

A Brahmin professor who saw the Swami very often in Madras after he had returned to India told me he noticed him going into little *samadhis* even while talking to people. From time to time his eyes would become absolutely still; then he would sigh deeply and become conscious of his surroundings again. I have heard that Swami Shivananda, who had gone to Madras to receive Swamiji, also mentioned this. In fact I myself learned from Swami Shivananda that after Swami Vivekananda returned from the West the first time he lived continually in the superconscious state. Yes, he had reached that high state, and there he remained. But these states are not good for the body. The body of even a pure soul is never equal to all these expressions and elevations of the spirit.

Yet exhausted and ill though he was, he worked continuously to establish the Indian work. Then in 1899 when it was set in good order, he once again, primarily for the sake of his health, left India for the West. He went first to England and very soon crossed to New York. Within a short time there was an occasion for him to come to Los Angeles.

3

Since I am concerned with San Francisco in this lecture, I won't dwell on Los Angeles too long. There was an

American disciple of the Swami's, Miss Josephine Mac-
Leod, who had been very loyal to him, and he had trust in
her strength, judgment, and goodness. She had come to
Los Angeles because her brother was very ill, and when
she entered the house where he was staying she was as-
tonished to see a big picture of Swami Vivekananda on
the wall. The owner of the house, a Mrs. Blodgett, had
heard the Swami in Chicago in 1893 and admired him
greatly. Miss MacLeod told her that she knew him and
had just left him in New York. In a few weeks the brother
died, and the two ladies persuaded the Swami to come to
Los Angeles as the guest of Mrs. Blodgett.

He arrived around the beginning of December, 1899,
and almost at once he felt he should teach. Like a lavish
spender he gave of his substance; he gave and gave and
gave. Many lectures he delivered in Los Angeles and in
nearby Pasadena. Transcripts of some of them have been
published in his *Complete Works,* and they are among
his finest.

There was a family of three sisters living in South
Pasadena. They had heard abut Swami Vivekananda's
talks at the Parliament of Religions and had read some
of his books; so when they learned from a newspaper
notice that he was to lecture in Los Angeles they went to
hear him, and of course their expectations were more
than realized. They took courage in hand, called on him
at Mrs. Blodgett's, and asked him to live in their home.
At first he refused. But one day he paid them a visit, and
after he had been in their house a little while he said, "I
shall live here with you; you can send for my things." He
told them he felt he had known all three before. Indeed,
he felt they were his own, and they, too, felt he was their

own. It might interest you to know that many years later the eldest of these sisters, Mrs. Wyckoff, gave her property in Hollywood to the Vedanta Society of Southern California, and that is where the Swami-in-Charge now lives. (The Southern California center has also acquired the house in South Pasadena where Swamiji stayed.) The youngest sister, Helen Mead, passed away while still young. The middle sister, Mrs. Hansbrough, did great service to the Swami, especially in San Francisco.

I shall tell you one interesting little story, though it may be a strain on your credulity. When he was about to leave Pasadena, Swamiji said to the sisters, "You know, it is my custom always to leave something of mine behind when I have lived in a place. So what shall it be?" He left his pipe on the mantelpiece. (He liked to smoke; that is not against spirituality.) Now, Mrs. Wyckoff used to suffer almost unbearable headaches, and in addition she had a great deal of personal anxiety. One day, long after the Swami had left, she had a very bad headache. She stood leaning on the mantelpiece and absently took that pipe in her hand and rubbed it on her forehead. As she did so, she heard the Swami's voice saying, "Madam, is it very hard to bear? It can't stay." Instantly all pain left her. The sisters kept this pipe as a sacred relic, not only because it was left by Swami Vivekananda but also because it was associated with such a strange happening.

The Swami stayed in southern California for almost three months and then came to San Francisco. His coming here seemed almost offhand. Once someone said to him, "Swami, you seem to be indifferent about your work. You don't take much into consideration. You just do things as they come to you." Some of his friends didn't like it; they thought everything should be planned and organized, pruned here and pasted there. But that was not his way. Mrs. Hansbrough later told me that she said to him one day, "Swami, I think if you go to San Francisco people will appreciate you more there." The Swami said, "Yes, they may." She said, "Would you like to go there? He said, "Yes, I might." But then the matter was dropped. A day or two later the Swami asked her, "Are you willing to go to San Francisco?" She was taken by surprise but said, "Yes, Swami, if you want." And thus the plan was made.

It so happened that a few days afterward the Swami received an invitation to come to northern California. The minister of the First Unitarian Church in Oakland, the Reverend Benjamin Fay Mills, wanted to hold a congress of religions in his church, which at the time was very well known. (It is still in existence, although that quarter of the city has now deteriorated.) Mr. Mills had attended the Parliament of Religions in Chicago and ever since had entertained great respect for Swami Vivekananda. Learning that he was in California, he invited him to speak at his congress, and the Swami agreed to come and talk on Vedanta. But he said to Mrs. Hansbrough, "Look here, you go and arrange for a lecture in San Francisco first." His idea was that he should start his work here independently.

So Mrs. Hansbrough came about a week ahead of him and made contacts with her acquaintances and friends, among them the leaders and members of the Home of Truth. As you may know, the Home of Truth was a religious organization similar in some respects to Chris-

tian Science and associated with the New Thought movement. At that time there were two Homes of Truth in
San Francisco—one on Pine Street and the other on California Street. Since the members had some appreciation
of Oriental philosophy, they were eager to welcome the
Swami and glad to give him a room and arrange for his
food in the Pine Street Home. He arrived there on the
evening of Thursday, February 22, 1900.

The next day he gave his first lecture, "The Ideal of a
Universal Religion," in Golden Gate Hall on Sutter Street.
Two days later he spoke at Mr. Mills' Congress of Religions, and from contemporary accounts I gather that a
huge crowd came to hear him. Both the church proper
and a large side hall were filled, and at least five hundred
people were turned away. He soon gave another lecture
at the Unitarian Church, and that too, was attended by
over two thousand people.

What effect the Swami's lectures had on the crowds
who heard them and how far they understood what they
heard is a question. Christ came and preached to the
multitudes, and even such a person—one who could
draw thousands, who could speak the wonderful words
of the Sermon on the Mount—reached very few. In fact,
so few were really impressed that the people didn't think
anything of his being crucified. Crowds are like this. The
state of the mass mind is very low and miserable. If
people were above the standard of the masses they would
not tolerate that state; but they find themselves in such
large company and they have such a comfortable life
with few disadvantages that they think this is the eternal axis of existence, nothing better exists; they are
locked up in this condition and their minds become com-

placent. Even if they hear something spiritual they don't want to hear it; it enters one ear and passes out the other. Nothing seems to leave an impression. Great souls come and preach to these masses but cannot shake them. The vast majority of church-goers come to the services, hear the sermon, put money in the collection box and go home the same persons. It is no different in India: millions bathe in the Ganges and go regularly to the temples but remain about the same. It is only through the pressure of society and unhappy experiences that the mind finds this existence is not so comfortable. Then a few try to get out and separate themselves from this huge mass. At first, of course, they seem lost; they are in a hopeless minority. Eventually, however, another keeps them company. That other is called God. Well, I hope I don't sound too cynical, but you see, when you think of these thousands of people who used to come and listen to the Swami you wonder how many were influenced by him.

But that is really not the important consideration. I would not care if not one person was impressed. I would not. What I care about is this: that a great mind like that of Swami Vivekananda exerted itself for the good of the people of this area. That is the most significant fact. You know, if someone told you, "The Lord in heaven is very much concerned about you," you would say, "What! The Lord Himself is concerned about me? Then I have nothing to worry about." Isn't it true? When a Swami Vivekananda becomes concerned about the people of an area, for centuries those who live there can say, "What a boon we have received! We have nothing to worry about." That is the way I look at it. You may think, "What arrant nonsense!" But I shall dedicate this morning to such nonsense. As I told you earlier, the Swami himself knew his power and effectiveness. On the last day of his life another monk overheard him say to himself, "If there were another Vivekananda, he would understand what I have done." At another time he said, "I have given enough for fifteen hundred years." He did not just deliver lectures; everything was charged with power. One word said casually by so great a soul, one small act, can produce tremendous activity for ages—this is the way things happen with the great.

And the Swami worked hard in this area. Through March and part of April he lectured in public halls in San Francisco and the East Bay almost every evening. In addition, he gave informal talks in private residences and in the Homes of Truth. Around the eighth of March he left the Pine Street Home of Truth and lived for a month in a rented flat on Turk Street, where Mrs. Hansbrough and another woman student kept house for him. In that flat he held a daily class on *raja yoga*, and many came to it. Generally the class began with meditation for fifteen to thirty minutes, but I have heard that on one occasion the Swami became so immersed in meditation that for an hour and a half he did not come out of it. Some of the students finally had to leave, but that was a most wonderful experience, to be seated near him at that time.

Unfortunately we have no full transcripts of Swami Vivekananda's lectures in the Bay Area; but nevertheless, we have the spirit of his teachings in San Francisco because a young woman, Miss Ida Ansell, took shorthand notes of many of the lectures he gave. She transcribed these notes in her old age. She herself told me how she came to hear the lectures. You see, she had hurt her hip and become crippled, and when she learned that a Miss Lydia Bell, the leader of the California Street Home of Truth, could cure people by the power of thought, she came and stayed with her. Then she met Swamiji. She was fascinated by him and by his lectures, but she was not interested so much in his teachings at that time as in Miss Bell's lessons and talks. Still, she went to almost all his lectures with Miss Bell and at some of them she took shorthand notes as an exercise. She told me she was afraid of Swamiji and that whenever she met him would move away from him. Well, you know, she was only twenty-two and not interested in his philosophy, and Swamiji was very impressive—awesome. She took down about twenty lectures as well as she could but never felt interested in transcribing them.

Years and years passed, and then in 1945 she came to San Francisco from Los Angeles for a vacation. That is when I met her for the first time. I said to her, "Since these lectures were given in San Francisco, it would be very nice if you would transcribe your notes; I am naturally interested to know what Swamiji said here." She agreed to try, and after she went back to Los Angeles she started. Every week or ten days she used to send me a transcription of one of the lectures until she had finished them all.

I had the good fortune of editing four of them. Then my health gave way, and I couldn't do this work, I felt, with proper faithfulness. You see there were many gaps in her notes, but as soon as I would read the transcripts the ideas that filled the gaps would at once rise in my mind; I had no difficulty in knowing what had been omitted. Maybe in one afternoon I would finish editing a lecture. When Miss Ansell saw these edited lectures she said, "Why, it seems as if I am hearing him! Everything seems to be as he said." Well, I was very much pleased. These four lectures were published in our magazine, *The Voice of India,* and later in the eighth volume of *The Complete Works of Swami Vivekananda.*

As it happened, 1 could do nothing further with the notes for a few years. In the meantime, in our Southern California center, where by this time she was living, Miss Ansell was urged to transcribe all her notes again, for she had kept no copies. She did this, and the remainder of the lectures came out in their magazine, *Vedanta and the West.* More recently they have been reprinted in the *Complete Works;* so now you can read many of Swami Vivekananda's San Francisco lectures and see the spirit they represent.

His last public lecture in San Francisco was given on the evening of April 14, 1900. A few days earlier, some of those who felt deeply attracted to him and to his teachings had asked him to organize a Vedanta Society here, and he had gladly agreed. So after that lecture a meeting was held for the purpose. That was the beginning of this present Society, which is now known as the Vedanta Society of Northern California. Although for a time the initial enthusiasm went down and only three or four members would come to the weekly meetings, the original group held together. Then gradually the center began to grow, and to this day it has continued to exist and grow in strength without a break.

4

Let me give you some details about the Swami when he lived here. I don't think his health was too bad; it was better than it had been in Los Angeles, where besides feeling ill he had been full of worries and anxieties about the monastery in India and how things were going there. But when he came to San Francisco, although there were still some difficulties to cause him anxiety, he seems to have been in a much better condition. In one of his letters he mentioned that he had wonderful sleep here, and whenever I think of it I feel very glad. All his life he had difficulty in sleeping, but if perchance he had a good sleep he would speak of that occasion for years as a red-letter day. He found walking helped him: he would take long walks in San Francisco, and although the hills bothered him at first, around the end of March he could write that he would "trudge" all over the city, uphill and down.

What was his appearance? Let us look at him. His complexion was quite fair for a Hindu, with a little golden tinge. He had luminous eyes—lotus petal eyes, as we say in India—and beautifully formed lips, a powerful jaw and a well-proportioned body. He was not very tall and leaned toward stoutness, but he was very majestic; he moved like a lion, particularly on the platform. The grace of his movement and his majesty gave many people the feeling that he was much taller than anyone around him. Sometimes one's mind gets caught up with the mental state of a person, and that person's body becomes as it were transformed. It is said his hair was jet black, not a single gray hair. When he arrived in Los Angeles he needed a haircut, but the sisters said, "You have such beautiful curly hair; we should hate to see it cut." So the Swami left it as it was. Some of the most beautiful photographs of him were taken in San Francisco, and they show his hair somewhat long, wavy, and parted in the middle.

His clothes were black—trousers and a long, gownlike coat according to Indian style, which he brought the second time he came to America for common use. On the platform and for formal occasions he wore a turban and a long robe tied with a sash. He used to carry them to lectures in a suitcase. His robe was a shade between orange and yellow, but he didn't care whether or not his turban matched it. I have seen among his effects as they are kept in our monastery turbans of different colors, some light salmon, others orange. As he spoke, his face, I have heard, would become animated, shining, and it blended wonderfully with his robe.

One rather irritating trait of his, but so sweet in him, was that he had no sense of time. If he was told he would miss the street car, he would say, "Don't hurry me. There will be another, won't there?" For one of his lectures in the Unitarian Church he was nearly an hour late. Hall crammed full, almost one hour gone—at a leisurely pace he came down the aisle. The audience had been noisily talking, but as the Swami majestically passed by, everybody fell silent. They forgot they had been waiting, such was his presence. Yes, if you are very thirsty you appreciate your glass of water more. One student said,"When I came to know him, I felt as if I had been waiting for him through the ages, and now I had found him!" At the sight of him people were just transported; his very appearance would remind them of the qualities of light and joy.

You may say, even so, unpunctuality is unpunctuality. Yes, that may be true. But to live in time was a bondage to the Swami. If you think a little carefully, you will find we have become prisoners of time. It is time that brings about nervous breakdowns and all kinds of troubles. If I have to finish my lecture in a short time, I shall just rush through it at four hundred words a minute (if that is possible). When you have to squeeze many things into a given period of time you must work at top speed, but the body was not made to stand that pace. Inherent conditions cannot really be changed; consequently you suffer. Swami Vivekananda was not bound by anything. He did not want to be caught in time, neither did he want to obey laws. He delighted in breaking stupid regulations. All in all he was quite informal.

His voice was very sweet. The manager of one of the halls where he spoke said, "I have heard many speakers, but never have I listened to such a sweet voice." It was between baritone and tenor, with a bell-like quality; not loud or powerful, and yet it could command a large audience. When he would recite Sanskrit verses, as he often did in the course of a lecture, quoting from the *Gita* or the Upanishads in illustration of his arguments, he would intone them, as is customary in India, and then translate them. I have heard that to listen to his Sanskrit recitation was one of the most beautiful experiences one could have. His pronunciation of English was perfect, with no foreign accent except for one or two words, and of course his devotees delighted in these variations.

Sometimes his lectures may have been too long—but

few minded. When he would rise in flights of expression of the highest truth, such was the quality of his presence that sometimes the whole audience would share in the true nature of the Self. It came so often that the Swami said many went into a sort of trance. Afterwards no doubt most of them would forget this experience, but for those few who were prepared for it, their lives were changed for good.

The Swami was infinitely gracious to certain people who sought his help. Why he gave more attention to some than to others one cannot know. It is said of great souls that they do things a little whimsically—they do not act in accordance with our calculations, and certainly he shared in this characteristic. There was a young woman living in Alameda who was in miserable health and had some mental difficulty. The first time she went to hear the Swami lecture she was tremendously attracted to him. She came the second time and approached him with great diffidence, not daring to speak to him, but he beckoned to her to come closer and said, "Madam, if you would like to see me privately, come to the flat tomorrow morning." She used to tell us, "All night long I just thought of questions to ask him. Early in the morning I went to the flat on Turk Street and was taken upstairs. He came into the room chanting softly and sat down across the room from me. All he said was, 'Well, Madam.' I could not speak but began to weep as though the flood gates had been opened. The Swami continued chanting for a while, then said, 'Come tomorrow about the same time.' All my questions were gone. All my troubles had vanished away." He was infinitely gracious to her. She used to come every day to his morning class, and afterwards he would sometimes let her help him cook. He was a wonderful cook—except that he was fond of hot red chilies and when he used them in his cooking others had to suffer the consequences. But when a Swami Vivekananda prepares a dish, even if it burns your mouth, it is a blessing.

I am telling you superficial things, really, but everything concerning him, even the most apparently insignificant thing—a gesture, a word, even a joke—seems to us to be laden with meaning, as it must be, because he did not live on this plane in which men live. His natural habitat was that transcendental consciousness in which the truth is eternally known and perceived. Everything that he said and did, therefore, is to us a revelation of that transcendental reality. There were undoubtedly times in which this transcendence was more manifest than at other times, but under no conditions did he live like an average man. And when he was in San Francisco he was living in a particularly high state. If an impure person gave him food, for instance, he instinctively knew he could not touch it. That happened here more than once. On one occasion an artist invited him to have dinner in Chinatown, but when the food was served, the Swami said, "No, I can't eat it." His host was heartbroken, and Swamiji explained, "The moment I looked at the cook I knew that if I ate the food I should throw it off. What is happening to me? I shall have to be kept in a glass cage if it continues." Also, around this time he could not touch money. If he did so, he would feel a painful electric shock. You know his Master, Sri Ramakrishna, would become unconscious in pain if money touched him. Swami Vivekananda began to feel the same thing.

Some of you may misunderstand. You have to know that the body of a spiritual man is different from that of an ordinary man. When one gains spiritual consciousness he cannot stand anything impure. He will not hate impurity, but as long as he lives in the relative world, the relative part of him reacts to it. It isn't a question of the body's health or illness; it is a question of the body's being an instrument of the Spirit. You read in the Bible about Christ touching a person and causing something tremendous to happen. If you say his mind did it all, then why did he touch with the body? No, the body of a spiritual person becomes something special. The power itself does not of course originate in the body; but it flows through the body, so that the body becomes changed, highly sensitized. The great ones, therefore, are very careful about it.

But as I was saying, the Swami was in a very high state while he was in San Francisco. This development may have begun before he left India the second time, but we do have more evidence of it in his San Francisco lectures, conversations, and letters, and to some extent in those of Los Angeles, than we find before he came to California. He had reached a point where he felt everything was just right; nothing had to be corrected. One day someone in Pasadena spoke to him of the evil in man and how man should be made good. "Madam," the Swami said—they were seated on a hilltop—"look at this handiwork of God. I like it all. I don't want to improve it. You say that man is also a product of God's hand—it is all His doing. How dare you say you want to improve on it?"

You might think, what a terrible teaching! Forget "teaching." Forget all this conventional way of looking at things without knowing why you do it. If God has actually created the bad man, why do you want to improve him? You can improve on God?

Miss Bell—she was a very nice person—made a statement of this same nature. She said, "This world is like a school where we learn lessons." The Swami laughed. "Who told you that? This isn't a school at all. It is a circus ring, and we are like clowns tumbling all over the ring. We don't have to learn anything here. We are already perfect. We like to tumble, that is all. When we get tired, we shall stop." Of course he didn't mean we are clowns in an ordinary sense. "You like to don the garb of a clown"— that is to say, you have taken the garb of a man, a woman, a poor man, a rich man. God Himself has taken all these forms. "Great fun, great fun!" he used to say. My friends, if you can catch even a little of this view of life, all your bondages will fall off, and you will at once become free.

His mind had reached a very high state of awareness about the world and about people. If you become spiritually conscious you find that slowly you pass through three stages. In the first stage you feel people are souls and not bodies, but some are advanced, some are not; some are spiritual, others worldly. In that consciousness you feel great compassion for men and want to help them by giving them knowledge of God. Most religious teachers and saints live in this state.

In the second stage there is this other consciousness: you see that all souls are really God Himself, perfect already; they don't have to be made perfect. Then what is it you will do? You will talk about this truth, but not in order to teach. You are not thinking, "Here is a weak and ignorant person; let me teach him." You feel the same perfect God manifesting in this infinite number of forms. That is a very high state of spiritual consciousness, in which there is no recognition that there are any bound souls or even that there is a material world. The whole thing you see to be pure divinity expressed in these infinite forms. You don't see differences: just as a friend looks different when he dresses differently, and you like him in all variations, so the same divinity expresses itself in all different forms. No question of high or low. In that state a person says, I am not here to improve anything. Swami Vivekananda was living in that consciousness.

The third state is that in which you are not aware of any variety at all. The manifold entirely disappears, and of what remains you can say nothing. This is the highest realization.

But the second stage is very close to the third. It is so high that unless the body and mind are properly trained, the body cannot contain it. You get glimpses of that state of Swamiji's mind when you read his letters of those days. He wrote the most beautiful letter to Miss MacLeod from the Alameda Home of Truth: "It is so still, so calm," he said, "and I am drifting, languidly, in the warm heart of the river. I dare not make a splash with my hands or feet for fear of breaking the wonderful stillness, stillness that makes you feel sure it is an illusion! Peace that one feels alone, surrounded with statues and pictures. The world *is*, but not beautiful nor ugly, but as sensations without exciting any emotion. Oh, the blessedness of it!

Everything is good and beautiful; for things are all losing
their relative proportions to me—my body among the
first."[4]

Of all who lived with him in the Turk Street flat, the
Alameda Home of Truth, or Camp Taylor I don't know
how many knew what was going on within him or felt
these profound realizations. His mood was that in which
paramahamsas and *avadhutas* live. Outwardly, their
lives are like the lives of common people, but inwardly
they are conscious only of ultimate truth—divinity. He
stayed in San Francisco in the mood of these liberated
ones. Such was the state of Swami Vivekananda's mind,
and in one sense it was reflected in the teachings he
imparted during this period.

5

The Swami's personality, which of course includes his
philosophical outlook, was exceedingly complex. People
read his lectures and come to various conclusions, and
when they bring these conclusions together they find
they don't blend at all. This has become a source of great
trouble to his students, and we who are timid people
naturally take the easiest course. If we cannot fit things
together we take scissors and lop off what we don't like
and say, "It's wonderfully harmonious. Now we understand." Many have done this. But I believe that if you
study his life from the time he came to his Master,
through those periods of wandering in India, of teaching
in the West, of returning to India and organizing his
work there, and of coming again to the West, you will find
that he was not the same throughout those years. There

was a subtle change in his teachings—a change in emphasis, an impatience with some ideas and a certain clarification of other ideas so that at last they stood out in bold outline.

We can say, I think, that the speaking and lecturing part of his mission was concluded in this city. After he left here he gave three or four short lectures in New York. We have only scanty notes of these. Then he spoke once or twice in Paris. After his return to India he went to the eastern part of Bengal and spoke twice there. And that is all. None of his lectures after he left San Francisco were of an outstanding nature. He really gave his final lectures here, and I consider that those lectures represent the highest development, the culmination, of his teachings. The Swami himself was heard to say during his stay in the Bay Region: "I have given my highest teachings in California."

It may not occur to you that he taught certain distinct things in California unless you have read all the lectures he gave and have thought about what he said in them. During his first visit to America he was certainly a roaring lion of Vedanta; there was more fire then, more inspiration; still, he did not tell people in so many words to think always that they are the Spirit, not the body, not the mind; he did not tell them to practice primarily *jnana yoga,* the path of knowledge. He taught, rather, that all four paths—knowledge, devotion, work, and meditation— are good and that any one of them, or a combination of two or more, will take you to the highest. But when he came to California he spoke more philosophically; his lectures were more serious from both a practical and a theoretical point of view. Here in San Francisco he said extraordinary things; he taught the highest *jnana*. Certainly the audiences here were very fortunate to have heard such high philosophy from his own lips. Even when you compare the lectures he gave in Los Angeles and Pasadena with those in San Francisco you find a difference: there was not so much emphasis on *jnana yoga* in southern California.

Let me come to the actual lectures Swami Vivekananda gave here, as far as we know of them. As I have said, we haven't a complete record of his lectures in the Bay Region; but of those we know, the subjects fall under three headings.

First there was a group of four lectures about the great religious teachers of the world—Christ, Buddha, Krishna, Mohammed. Two of these were unique: he had not given a full lecture anywhere else on Sri Krishna, nor do we find among his published lectures any other on Mohammed. Unfortunately we have no transcript or report of the Swami's San Francisco lecture on Christ. However, we do have a transcript of his Los Angeles lecture "Christ the Messenger," which was one of his most beautiful.

All these talks are precious to us. We certainly want to know what a man like Swami Vivekananda thought about these great teachers, and here we find his understanding of them and his devotion to them incomparable. He concluded one of these lectures by saying, "Glory unto the great souls whose lives we have been studying! They are the living gods of the world. . . . We can only see Him if He takes the limitation of man. . . . Therefore, salutations unto you, . . . leaders of the human race! Salutations unto you, great teachers! You leaders have our salutations for ever and ever."[5]

The second group of lectures was concerned with spiritual practice. It included such titles as "Formal Worship," "Breathing," "Meditation," "Concentration." He spoke a great deal on practical spirituality, and as part of his practical teaching he laid great stress on the need for manliness—strength. I have noticed that the biographers of Swami Vivekananda, perhaps on the basis of the titles in this second group, have made the mistake of saying that he spoke particularly on *raja yoga* in San Francisco. This is not at all true. Even his lectures that dealt with *raja yoga* were characterized by the element which predominated in all his teachings here—his emphasis on the glory of man's true Self.

The lectures of the third group were directly concerned with this teaching. In these he told vital and direct truths about everything to everyone in the most forceful language he could find. Some of the titles of this group are, "I Am That I Am," "Discipleship," "Is Vedanta the Future Religion?" "The Soul and God," "The Goal." Many of you must have read "Is Vedanta the Future Religion?" which is published in volume eight of the Swami's *Complete Works*. I have felt it is something special. It contains many things he did not say in other lectures, certainly not with the same emphasis and strength. Undoubtedly, it was a bombshell exploded in the face of hundreds. He used to use that expression: once at the end of a lecture he said, "Come tomorrow. I shall throw a bombshell. Come on, it will do you good!" In this lecture he certainly threw a bombshell.

He went straight to the heart of the matter. He saw this most profound truth—that the nature of man is identical with the ultimate divine Reality, and he wanted man to wake up to this truth of his own being. He didn't bother here about any other kinds of religion. He was a great devotee of God, yet he said, "Throw this old gentleman away!" "You are the Personal God. If you want a Personal God, *you* are that God." Why did he say those things? You see what a miserable situation mankind is in; religion ought to be doing a much better job than it has done so far. Why has it failed? Because it has neglected the most important truth and emphasized things which are unimportant. The most important truth is the truth about my Self—your Self. That is the profound truth. If I start by thinking I am an ignorant and sinful man, how can I love God? How can I have the strength and courage to go through all the practices necessary for religion? That is why the Swami spoke in such strong language. Be aware of your true Self first; know your own truth first! Unless you do that, you have no hope. That is one perfectly new thing he gave.

Almost all the Swami's lectures in San Francisco were exploding bombshells. He did not get excited; yet he was most powerful and uncompromising. Free person that he was, he had no concern for the opinion of others. He used to say things that startled people. There was no fear, no compromising of truth, no thinking what people liked. After a lecture in Oakland someone asked him whether he was married. He said, "No! Why should I be married? Marriage is the devil's own game." It was certainly a startling thing to say to married people—most uncompromising.

There was no mincing matters at all. Here in San Francisco he said very clearly: "Throw off the Personal God and these churches. They have accomplished nothing. They haven't done any good. Come out of the churches! No laying of flowers on the altar. Throw all that away. That is not worship; that is not religion." Some of you will say, "How can it be? He is saying something that is against the teachings of all other spiritual leaders. Sri Ramakrishna himself did not say that." But remember this: When Sri Ramakrishna worshiped in the temple and offered flowers, he did it with his whole heart. He said, "I *must* find God." When you feel like that, whatever you do is as deep as God-realization. But when we worship with no real yearning for God, it becomes just a binding formality. Such formalism goes on for ages. Great teachers come and teach the truth, and because their fiery truth scorches us, we allow it to go out, and very soon it becomes a handful of ashes. We become bound in church formality, and that is all.

Until now in the history of religion there has been the doctrine that you should tell people only those things which are in accordance with their understanding. Don't tell those who are not advanced about advanced things; they will be hurt. Even in India this has been so. It is the doctrine of *adhikara*, the doctrine of fitness. Shortly before coming West the second time, Swami Vivekananda said at the Belur Math, "The time has come when all truths should be given to all people unobstructedly and without compromise." Yes, it will hurt at first. But do you think by not telling people the truth you will spare them from being hurt? Later they will be hurt by lack of truth. Swami Vivekananda followed that principle here in San Francisco. He taught the highest truths to the common man, truths which heretofore great teachers have not given even to the qualified.

Why do you think the Swami said all truths should be given to everyone? Simply because he was carried away by his own ideas? No. Remember that he was a profound student of the human mind and of history. He had encyclopedic knowledge, and, as I mentioned earlier, he claimed that he could see the future for three hundred years spread before him in detail. He knew which way men were going. And isn't it towards truth that you are going? How can truth really hurt you? We get into all kinds of ruts of thought and make little patterns and molds for ourselves and continually cast our lives in them. All this antiquated stuff! Aren't new ways possible? How do you know this is the best your mind is capable of? Because some ancient people did something, you think nothing better can be done? Then why don't you go on living in dirty old caves instead of skyscrapers? In everything else you believe in progress, in everything else—in all the sciences—you are seeking truth, but when it comes to religion, you think you must believe in what a man taught thousands of years ago; you think nothing else is possible.

But in this age it is absolutely necessary to learn that the one truth is that man is Spirit. That is the teaching Swami Vivekananda emphasized here again and again, again and again. Such are the circumstances of life now that whether we like it or not we are forced to look into our own Self. Have you anything you can call your own? Your family, your fortune, your future, nothing is secure; you do not know what is going to happen from day to day. And that is true in every part of the world. Our personality is gone. We have lost our bearings. Even in religion the old forms and beliefs are going whether we like it or not; old landmarks are going, and they will continue to go. What will give you a sense of security and wholeness? Can you find happiness in being kicked around by circumstances? No, something within you will cry for independence, and that will be the recognition of your own spiritual Self. If you can discover It, recognize It, then, though the whole world swirls around you, you will still feel yourself the Lord of circumstances. If you haven't discovered It, you are gone.

So I say, circumstances themselves are forcing us to recognize our true nature. Gods or saviours will not avail. They have not. You see it before your eyes. In Bengal within a year about six million people died of famine. How many more will die of disease we do not know. Bengal is full of temples and people ringing bells. Where were the gods? What happened to the gods in those dire hours?

If you remind me that destruction is also a gift of God, very good, but then let us be strong. If we have a God who gives us a stone when we ask for bread, then let us be the kind of people who are able to eat stone. We cannot be those gentle, devout, soft souls, expecting God to be always kind and compassionate. He does not act that way. Let us recognize that fact, and all weakness will fall off. Devotees become strong when they can say, "Give me happiness, give me misery, both I shall accept with extreme gladness." But those who say, "Oh God, give me fur coats, give me seventy degrees of heat, give me health, You are so kind, You are great!" will never find peace; for there *is* no such God, and their belief in such a God will betray them. Weakness will never prevail. Therefore become strong.

Our heart in its weakness is continually drawn to a soft picture of the Ultimate Reality. We want to look at a kind Personal God and to feel reassured. But again and again Swami Vivekananda said: "No, there is no help for you. No one can help you; God cannot help you; no one. You alone can help yourself." When you think your prayers are being answered, it is your own hidden Self working from within that answers them. He said that not only here in San Francisco, but in other places as well—London, for example. And, my friends, isn't there much greater hope in the thought that you have infinite power within you than in the thought that you are a helpless creature dependent upon a God who sometimes gives you what you want and sometimes does not? Swami Vivekananda did not bother about whether God gives or does not give. No; he said, "*You* are the Personal God. Every man is a Personal God."

Now of course that is a very big thing. If you use the word God in the sense of the Creator, Maintainer, Destroyer and then say, I am that God, it would seem like very big talk. But there is another sense in which you can say I am God: The king's son is also royal. He cannot rule the kingdom, he has not inherited the throne yet, but royal blood runs through his veins, he is someone separate from the common man. So in that sense you can say, "My true nature, the truth about me, the reality of me, is Divinity; it is not body or mind." It was in this sense that the Swami said, "You are the Spirit, you are the Personal God; if you want to talk about Personal God, *you* are that Personal God."

It should not be difficult for you to think those things; it is just perversity that you do not want to. In "Discipleship" the Swami said, "In one moment you can become free!" Why do I have to say that I am a limited being and a sinner, a body and a mind—all of which are falsehoods? Why should I not say—whether I perceive it or not—that my nature is divine? If I am blind and deny there is any furniture in my room, is this true just because I don't see the furniture? Do I have to accept everything that breeds fear, limitation, and all these miseries just because I won't pay attention to the truth? It is not true to say that I have *forgotten* the truth; no, deliberately I don't pay attention to it. Isn't it strange? Knowing this is the truth, we still say in the same breath, "It must take years and years before we realize the truth." Why not say at once, "I am That"?—and there's an end to it. You are convinced intellectually, but then you behave as if you had not been convinced at all; you follow something false. Swami Vivekananda did not like that. He himself wanted to rise to where time is not, nor circumstance, where truth is shining, and he was equally impatient for everyone to go there and to be there.

You might bring in your arguments here, as others have done: "Oh, no, no, no, that's not practical! Oh, no, no, no! You cannot expect all people to practice these things; they are so attached to their bodies, their wives and husbands, their children, their this, their that. They cannot practice meditation many hours a day." You will also say that a person has to have intellect to practice monistic Vedanta. Yes, that is true. But it is not so impracticable as you think. It is the monists themselves who have done the greatest mischief.Anyone who talks about monism, anyone who wants to say, I am the Spirit, they will discourage: "Oh, he is not real; he only talks." In the path of devotion all of you are real from the very beginning? You cry out, "I am the servant of God." You are the servant of God!—the most selfish person I ever met in my life. It will take many, many births in this path before you can become even a fragment of a servant of God. Do you think even in dualism or the devotional path you become real just because you shout out words or because you dance around and shed lots of tears? We know that those who shed too many tears are hypocrites. My friends, any path is difficult if your heart is not in it. If you are serious, what path you follow is of little importance.

But if you follow monism, you will get quick results; that is what Swami Vivekananda's contention was. And he wanted people to be strong, standing on their two strong feet, depending upon none. He wanted us at the very first to go to our own true nature. Work from that. Such a religion at once calls for a transcendental attitude about things. When you first learn that man is Spirit, you are at once lifted up. After having learned that, love God and serve man, but first of all rise there. If you don't, all the other things you do will be so superficial that they will not avail. This is the great teaching Swami Vivekananda gave in San Francisco. Again and again he came back to that, again and again with tremendous strength and emphasis he would return to the theme of the true nature of man.

Well, how could it have been otherwise? When I think of the especially high state he was in, I understand why he lectured in the way he did here—why he didn't say, "Acquire a little devotion. You should not think you are Brahman." How could he talk in that language? Even a small man like myself is convinced that everyone is divine, and he who used to see that truth shining before his eyes all the time, how could he have taught anything else?

But remember, this was not just monism as taught by Shankara and others. Yes, he taught many things in common with them; but if you want to interpret Swami Vivekananda's Vedanta by saying it is a repetition of the old philosophies, you will miss his most essential teachings. He taught Advaita, but did he teach that alone? What do you understand by Advaita, nondual Vedanta? You have a stereotyped idea of the paths of *karma, jnana, bhakti,* and *yoga.* He taught all the paths and the Advaita that belongs to all the paths. Who, for instance, can love God more than he who is Godlike? Only when you know you are Spirit can you have true devotion for God, the Spirit. You will feel that He is close to you, He is identified with you, He is your very own. Then moments will come when you feel that even the little remaining sense of duality disappears. That is the *bhakti* he taught here. He has thrown new light on the paths of devotion, action, concentration, knowledge, on human life, on the human mind.

In the last analysis, as he himself said, he didn't teach any "ism" at all. He wanted to wake man up to the truth of his own being—that is all. My friends, only when we have awakened to the deeper understanding of our own Self shall we understand what devotion truly means, what action truly means, what meditation and concentration truly mean; and only then shall we truly understand all that Swami Vivekananda taught.

But I am very glad to say this: I see that millions and

millions of men and women by force of circumstances are being compelled to throw off the old ideas that have kept them in darkness and ignorance generation after generation, incarnation after incarnation, and to recognize their deeper nature. The various needs of people—spiritual as well as earthly—will compel them to take up the religion Swami Vivekananda preached and to which he gave his boldest, most uncompromising expression here in San Francisco. Through strength, through fearlessness man, in every part of the world, will have to rise to his feet and do things that have been neglected for centuries and centuries, things we cannot any longer ignore or forget. Then we will feel that here was the man who came with the word for us and that his word is our guide. It is the light we shall follow.

Before I conclude, I would like to accent one special aspect of his stay here which is fortunate for us. As you know, this Society has a retreat near Olema in Marin County. Not far from there—about ten minutes' drive— is the campsite Swami Vivekananda went to in May of 1900. It is now a part of the Samuel Taylor State Park and can be visited. It is among tall redwoods on the right side of the road to Olema as you cross the first bridge over Papermill Creek. The Swami stayed in this camp for more than two weeks with Miss Bell, Mrs. Hansbrough, Miss Ansell, and another student, a Mrs. Roorbach. Every day they meditated under the trees, and then for hours the Swami would talk about God. He was not in good health, having lectured every day—sometimes twice a day—for many weeks; the little health he had gained in California was gone. A ticket had been bought for him to go to Chicago in the beginning of May, but when his students found that his health was so bad they proposed that he go to this camp instead. It is indeed a sacred spot. Just imagine that spot where for so many days he meditated and had God-realization! Where are the places, in any country, where a man has seen God? It was because of the sacredness of that spot and in memory of his stay there, that we secured our retreat so close by..

After this vacation he went to Chicago and New York, and from New York he went to Paris. In the late fall of 1900 he traveled through Europe to Constantinople and then to Egypt, where he took a boat to India. And within two years he passed away.

You see, he crossed our sky like a powerful comet—a visitation from the unknown blazed across the sky of our life. It was so brilliant, so full of hope for one and all, that forever it will remain shining before our eyes to draw us towards it until we too have become dwellers in the realm of light.

References

1. *The Complete Works of Swami Vivekananda* (Calcutta: Advaita Ashrama, 1973), vol. 5 (10th ed.), p. 314.
2. *See* Sister Nivedita, *The Master as I Saw Him,* 10th edition (Calcutta: Udbodhan Office, 1966), p. 31.
3. *See* ibid, p. 164.
4. *Complete Works,* vol. 6 (9th ed.) p. 433.
5. Ibid., vol. 1 (1st subsidized ed.) p. 445.

Extracts from Lectures
of Swami Vivekananda
Delivered in
San Francisco, 1900

Extracts from Lectures of Swami Vivekananda

From "Discipleship"

It is not easy to be a disciple; great preparations are necessary; many conditions have to be fulfilled. . . .The first condition is that the student who wants to know the truth must give up all desires for gain in this world or in the life to come.

The truth is not what we see. What we see is not truth as long as any desire creeps into the mind. God is true, and the world is not true. So long as there is in the heart the least desire for the world, truth will not come. Let the world fall to ruin around my ears: I do not care. So with the next life; I do not care to go to heaven. What is heaven? Only the continuation of this earth. We could be better and the little foolish dreams we are dreaming would break sooner if there were no heaven, no continuation of this silly life on earth. By going to heaven we only prolong the miserable illusions.

What do you gain in heaven? You become gods, drink nectar, and get rheumatism. There is less misery there than on earth, but also less truth. The very rich can understand truth much less than the poorer people. . . . The rich rarely become religious. Why? Because they think if they become religious they will have no more fun in life. In the same way there is very little chance to become religious in heaven; there is too much comfort and enjoyment there—the dwellers in heaven are disinclined to give up their fun.

They say there will be no more weeping in heaven. I do not trust the man who never weeps; he has a big block of granite where the heart should be. It is evident that the heavenly people have not much sympathy. There are vast masses of them over there, and we are miserable creatures suffering in this horrible place. They could pull us all out of it; but they do not. They do not weep. There is no sorrow or misery there; therefore they do not care for anyone's misery. They drink their nectar, dances go on; beautiful wives and all that.

Going beyond these things, the disciple should say, "I do not care for anything in this life nor for all the heavens that have ever existed—I do not care to go to any of them. I do not want the sense-life in any form, this identification of myself with the body as I feel now—'I am this body, this huge mass of flesh.' This is what I feel I am. I refuse to believe that."

The world and the heavens, all these are bound up with the senses. You do not care for the earth if you do not have any senses. Heaven also is the world. Earth, heaven, and all that is between have but one name—earth.

Therefore the disciple, knowing the past and the present and thinking of the future, knowing what prosperity means, what happiness means, gives up all these and seeks to know the truth and truth alone. This is the first condition.

From "Is Vedanta the Future Religion?"

I shall begin by telling you what Vedanta is not, and then I shall tell you what it is. But you must remember that with all its emphasis on impersonal principles, Vedanta is not antagonistic to anything, though it does not compromise or give up the truths which it considers fundamental. . . .

First, [Vedanta] does not believe in a book—that is the difficulty to start with. It denies the authority of any book over any other book. It denies emphatically that any one book can contain all the truths about God, soul, the ultimate reality. Those of you who have read the Upanishads remember that they say again and again, "Not by the reading of books can we realize the Self."

Second, [Vedanta] finds veneration for some particular person still more difficult to uphold. Those of you who are students of Vedanta—by Vedanta is always meant the Upanishads—know that this is the only religion that does not cling to any person. Not one man or woman has ever become the object of worship among the Vedantins. . . .

A still greater difficulty is about God. You want to be democratic in this country. It is the democratic God that Vedanta teaches. . . . Its God is not the monarch sitting on a throne, entirely apart. There are those who like their God that way—a God to be feared and propitiated. They burn candles and crawl in the dust before Him. They want a king to rule them—they believe in a king in heaven to rule them all. The king is gone from this country [America] at least. Where is the king of heaven now? Just where the earthly king is. In this country the king has entered every one of you. You are all kings in this country. So with the religion of Vedanta. You are all Gods. One God is not sufficient. You are all Gods, says the Vedanta.

This makes Vedanta very difficult. It does not teach

the old idea of God at all. In place of that God who sat above the clouds and managed the affairs of the world without asking our permission, who created us out of nothing just because He liked it and made us undergo all this misery just because He liked it, Vedanta teaches the God that is in everyone, has become everyone and everything. His majesty the king has gone from this country; the Kingdom of Heaven went from Vedanta hundreds of years ago. . . .There is a chance of Vedanta becoming the religion of your country because of democracy. But it can become so only if you can and do clearly understand it, if you become real men and women, not people with vague ideas and superstitions in your brains, and if you want to be truly spiritual, since Vedanta is concerned only with spirituality. . . .

God is Spirit and He should be worshipped in Spirit and in truth. Does Spirit live only in heaven? What is Spirit? We are all Spirit. Why is it we do not realise it? What makes you different from me? Body and nothing else. Forget the body, and all is Spirit.

These are what Vedanta has not to give. No book. No man to be singled out from the rest of mankind—"You are worms, and we are the Lord God!"—none of that. If you are the Lord God, I also am the Lord God. So Vedanta knows no sin. There are mistakes, but no sin; and in the long run everything is going to be all right. No Satan—none of this nonsense. Vedanta believes in only one sin, only one in the world, and it is this: the moment you think you are a sinner or anybody is a sinner, that is sin. From that follows every other mistake or what is usually called sin. There have been many mistakes in our lives. But we are going on. Glory be onto us that we have made mistakes! Take a long look at your past life. If your present condition is good, it has been caused by all the past mistakes as well as successes. Glory be unto mistakes! Do not look back upon what has been done. Go ahead!

You see, Vedanta proposes no sin nor sinner. No God to be afraid of. He is the one Being of whom we shall never be afraid, because He is our own Self. There is only one being of whom you cannot possibly be afraid; He is that. Then is not he really the most superstitious person who has fear of God? There may be someone who is afraid of his shadow; but even he is not afraid of himself. God is man's very Self. He is that one being whom you can never possibly fear. What is all this nonsense, the fear of the Lord entering into a man, making him tremble and so on? Lord bless us that we are not all in the lunatic asylum! But if most of us are not lunatics, why should we invent such ideas as fear of God? Lord Buddha said that the whole human race is lunatic, more or less. It is perfectly true, it seems. . . .

What does Vedanta teach us? In the first place, it teaches that you need not even go out of yourself to know the truth. All the past and all the future are here in the present. No man ever saw the past. Did any one of you see the past? When you think you are knowing the past, you only imagine the past in the present moment. To see the future, you would have to bring it down to the present, which is the only reality—the rest is imagination. This present is all that is. There is only the One. All is here right now. One moment in infinite time is quite as complete and all-inclusive as every other moment. All that is and was and will be is here in the present. Let anybody try to imagine anything outside of it—he will not succeed. . . .

We shall understand this by and by, and then see it: all the heavens—everything—are here, now, and they really are nothing but appearances on the Divine Presence. This Presence is much greater than all the earths and heavens. People think that this world is bad and imagine that heaven is somewhere else. This world is not bad. It is God Himself if you know it. It is a hard thing even to understand, harder, then, to believe. The murderer who is going to be hanged tomorrow is all God, perfect God. It is very hard to understand, surely; but it can be understood.

Therefore Vedanta formulates not universal brotherhood, but universal oneness. I am the same as any other man, as any animal—good, bad, anything. It is one body, one mind, one soul throughout. Spirit never dies. There is no death anywhere, not even for the body. Not even the mind dies. How can even the body die? One leaf may fall—does the tree die? The universe is my body. See how it continues. All minds are mine. Through all mouths I speak. In everybody I reside. . . .

What is the God of Vedanta? He is principle, not person. You and I are all Personal Gods. The absolute God of the universe, the creator, preserver, and destroyer of the universe is impersonal principle. You and I, the cat, rat, devil, and ghost—all these are Its persons—all are Personal Gods. You want to worship Personal Gods? It is the worship of your own Self. . . .

God is the infinite, impersonal Being—ever existent, unchanging, immortal, fearless; and you are all His incarnations, His embodiments. This is the God of Vedanta, and His heaven is everywhere. In this heaven dwell all the Personal Gods there are—you yourselves. . . .

Worship everything as God—every form is His temple. All else is delusion. Always look within, never without. Such is the God that Vedanta preaches, and such is His worship. Naturally there is no sect, no creed, no caste in Vedanta. . . .

If Vedanta—this conscious knowledge that all is one Spirit—spreads, the whole of humanity will become spiritual. But is it possible? I do not know. Not within thousands of years. The old superstitions must run out. You are all interested in how to perpetuate all your superstitions. Then there are the ideas of the family brother, the caste brother, the national brother. All these are barriers to the realisation of Vedanta. Religion has been religion to very few. . . .

There is another side to the question. Everyone says that the highest, the pure truth cannot be realised all at once by all, that men have to be led to it gradually through worship, prayer, and other kinds of prevalent religious practices. I am not sure whether that is the right method or not. . . .

Sometimes I agree that there is some good in the dualistic method; it helps many who are weak.... But then I think of the other side. How long will the world have to wait to reach the truth if it follows this slow, gradual process? How long? And where is the surety that it will ever succeed to any appreciable degree? It has not so far. After all, gradual or not gradual, easy or not easy to the weak, is not the dualistic method based on falsehood? Are not all the prevalent religious practices often weakening and therefore wrong? They are based on a wrong idea, a wrong view of man. Would two wrongs make one right? Would the lie become truth? Would darkness become light?. . . .

For thousands of years millions and millions all over the world have been taught to worship the Lord of the world, the Incarnations, the saviours, the prophets. They have been taught to consider themselves helpless, miserable creatures and to depend upon the mercy of some person or persons for salvation. There are no doubt many marvellous things in such beliefs. But even at their best, they are but kindergartens of religion, and they have helped but little. Men are still hypnotised into abject degradation. However, there are some strong souls who get over that illusion. The hour comes when great men will arise and cast off these kindergartens of religion and make vivid and powerful the true religion, the worship of the Spirit by the Spirit.

From "I Am That I Am"

Everything is substance plus name and form. Name and form come and go, but substance remains ever the same....Nature is time, space, and causation. Nature is name and form. Nature is Maya. Maya means name and form, into which everything is cast. Maya is not real. We could not destroy it or change it if it were real. The substance is noumenon; Maya is phenomenon. There is the real "me" which nothing can destroy, and there is the phenomenal "me" which is continually changing and disappearing.

The fact is, everything existing has two aspects. One is noumenal, unchanging and indestructible; the other is phenomenal, changing and destructible. Man in his true nature is substance, soul, Spirit. This soul, this Spirit never changes, is never destroyed; but it appears to be clothed with a form and to have a name associated with it. This form and name are not immutable or indestructible; they continually change and are destroyed. Yet men foolishly seek immortality in this changeable aspect, in the body and mind—they want to have an eternal body. I do not want that kind of immortality.

What is the relation between me and nature? In so far as nature stands for name and form or for time, space, and causality, I am not part of nature, because I am free, I am immortal, I am unchanging and infinite. The question does not arise whether I have free will or not; I am beyond any will at all. Wherever there is will, it is never free. There is no freedom of will whatever. There is freedom of that which becomes will when name and form get hold of it, making it their slave. That substance—the soul—as it were molds itself, as it were throws itself into the cast of name and form, and immediately becomes bound, whereas it was free before. And yet its original nature is still there. That is why it says, "I am free; in spite of all this bondage, I am free." And it never forgets this.

But when the soul has become the will, it is no more really free. Nature pulls the strings, and it has to dance as nature wants it to. Thus have you and I danced throughout the years. All the things that we see, do, feel, know, all our thoughts and actions are nothing but dancing to the dictates of nature. There has been, and there is, no freedom in any of this. From the lowest to the highest, all thoughts and actions are bound by law, and none of these pertain to our real Self.

My true Self is beyond all law. Be in tune with slavery, with nature, and you live under law, you are happy under law. But the more you obey nature and its dictates, the more bound you become; the more in harmony with ignorance you are, the more you are at the beck and call of everything in the universe. Is this harmony with nature, this obedience to law, in accord with the true nature and destiny of man? What mineral ever quarreled with and disputed any law? What tree or plant ever defied law? This table is in harmony with nature, with law; but a table it remains always, it does not become any better. Man begins to struggle and fight against nature. He makes many mistakes, he suffers. But eventually he conquers nature and realises his freedom. When he is free, nature becomes his slave.

The awakening of the soul to its bondage and its effort to stand up and assert itself—this is called life. Success in this struggle is called evolution. The eventual triumph, when all the slavery is blown away, is called salvation, Nirvana, freedom. Everything in the universe is struggling for liberty. When I am bound by nature, by name and form, by time, space, and causality, I do not know what I truly am. But even in this bondage my real Self is not completely lost. I strain against the bonds; one by one they break, and I become conscious of my innate grandeur. Then comes complete liberation. I attain to the clearest and fullest consciousness of myself—I know that I am the infinite Spirit, the master of nature, not its slave. Beyond all differentiation and combination, beyond space, time, and causation, I am that I am.

From "The Soul and God"

Do not say "God"; do not say "Thou." Say "I." The language of dualism says "God, Thou, my Father." The language of nondualism says, "Dearer unto me than I am myself. I would have no name for Thee. The nearest I can use is 'I'.

"God is true. The universe is a dream. Blessed am I that I know this moment that I have been and shall be free [for] all eternity, that I know that I am worshipping only myself, that no nature, no delusion, had any hold on me. Vanish nature from me, vanish these gods, vanish worship; vanish superstitions, for I know my Self. I am the Infinite. All these—Mrs. So-and-so, Mr. So-and so, responsibility, happiness, misery— have vanished I am the Infinite. How can there be death for me, or birth? Whom shall I fear? I am the One. Shall I be afraid of myself? Who is to be afraid of whom? I am the one Existence. Nothing else exists. I am everything."

It is only a question of remembering your true nature; it is not salvation by work. Do you *get* salvation? You are already free.

Go on saying, "I am free." Never mind if the next moment delusion comes and says, "I am bound." Dehypnotise the whole thing.

This truth is first to be heard. Hear it first. Think on it day and night. Fill the mind with it day and night: "I am It. I am the Lord of the universe. Never was there any delusion." Meditate upon it with all the strength of the mind till you actually see these walls, houses— everything melt away; until body, everything, vanishes. "I will stand alone. I am the One." Struggle on! "Who cares? We want to be free; we do not want any powers. Worlds we renounce; heavens we renounce; hells we renounce. What do I care about all these powers and this and that? What do I care if the mind is controlled or uncontrolled? Let it run on! What of that! I am not the mind. Let it go on!"

The sun shines on the just and the unjust. Is God

touched by the defective character of anyone? "I am He.
Whatever my mind does, I am not touched. The sun is
not touched by shining on filthy places; I am Existence."

This is the religion of nondual philosophy. It is difficult. Struggle on! Down with all superstitions! Neither
teachers nor scriptures nor gods exist. Down with
temples, with priests, with gods, with incarnations, with
God Himself! I am all the God that ever existed! There,
stand up, philosophers! No fear! Speak no more of God
and the superstition of the world. Truth alone triumphs,
and this is true: I am the Infinite.

. . .Just see what it takes to become a philosopher!
This is the path of *jnana-yoga,* the way through knowledge. The other paths are easy, slow, but this is pure
strength of mind. No weakling can follow this path of
knowledge. You must be able to say: "I am the Soul, the
ever free; I never was bound. Time is in me, not I in time.
God was born in my mind. God the Father, Father of the
universe, He is created by me in my own mind."

Do you call yourselves philosophers? Show it! Think
of this, talk of this, and help each other in this path. Give
up all superstition!

From "The Goal"

Nature is conquered by man every day. As a race, man
is manifesting his power. Try in imagination to put a
limit to this power in man. You admit that man as a race
has infinite power, has an infinite body. The only question
is what you are. Are you the race or one individual? The
moment you isolate yourself, everything hurts you. The

moment you expand and feel for others, you gain help. The selfish man is the most miserable in the world. The happiest is the man who is not at all selfish. He has become the whole creation, the whole race, and God is within him. So in dualism—Christian, Hindu, and all religions—the code of ethics is: Do not be selfish. Be unselfish. Do things for others! Expand! . . .

The truth is, you are not separate from this universe. . . . Our bodies are little whirlpools in the ocean of matter. Life is taking a turn and passing on in another form. The sun, the moon, the stars, you and I are mere whirlpools. Why did I select a particular mind as mine? It is simply a mental whirlpool in the ocean of mind. . . .

The whole universe is composed of time, space, and causation. And God appears as this universe. When did nature begin? When you forgot your true nature and became bound by time, space, and causation. . . .Time began when you began to think. Space began when you got the body; otherwise there cannot be any space. Causation began when you became limited. If we have to have a certain sort of answer, there is the answer [—causation.] [But all this] is just play. Just for the fun of it. Nothing binds you; nothing forces you. You were never bound. We are all acting our parts in this play of our own invention.

But let us bring another question about individuality. Some people are so afraid of losing their individuality! . . .We must first understand what is meant by individuality. It is attaining the ideal. You are man now—or you are woman. You will change all the time. Can you stop? Do you want to keep your minds as they are now—the angers, hatreds, jealousies, quarrels, all the thousand and one things in the mind? Do you mean to say that you will keep them? You cannot stop anywhere until perfect conquest has been achieved, until you are pure and you are perfect.

You have no more anger when you are all love, bliss, infinite existence. Which of your bodies will you keep? You cannot stop anywhere until you come to life that never ends. Infinite life! You stop there. You have a little knowledge now and are always trying to get more. Where will you stop? Nowhere, until you become one with life itself.

Many want pleasure as the goal. For that pleasure they seek only the senses. On the higher planes much pleasure is to be sought. Then on spiritual planes. Then in himself—God within him. The man whose pleasure is outside of himself becomes unhappy when that outside thing goes. You cannot depend for this pleasure upon anything in this universe. If all my pleasures are in myself, I must have pleasure there all the time because I can never lose my Self. Mother, father, child, wife, body, wealth—everything I can lose except my Self, bliss in the Self. All desire is contained in the Self. This is individuality which never changes, and this is perfect. . . .

And how to get it? . . . What are we to do to be free? Free you are already. How could the free ever be bound? It is a lie. You were never bound. How could the unlimited ever be limited by anything? Infinite divided by infinite, added to infinite, multiplied by infinite, remains infinite. You are infinite; God is infinite. You are all infinite. There cannot be two existences, only one. The Infinite can never be made finite. You are never bound. That is all. You are free already. You have reached the goal—all there is to reach. Never allow the mind to think that you have not reached the goal.

Whatever we think, that we become. If you think you are poor sinners, you hypnotise yourselves: "I am a miserable, crawling worm." Those who believe in hell are in hell when they die; those who say that they will go to heaven, go to heaven.

It is all play. You may say, "We have to do something; let us do good." Who cares for good and evil? Play! God Almighty plays. That is all. You are the almighty God playing....It is all fun. Know it and play. That is all there is to it. Then practice it. The whole universe is a vast play. All is good because all is fun. This star comes and crashes with our earth, and we are all dead. That too is fun. You only think fun the little things that delight your senses. . . .

I am in the sun, the moon, and the stars. I am with God, and I am in all the gods. I worship my Self.

There is another side to it. I have kept it in reserve. I am the man that is going to be hanged. I am all the wicked. I am getting punished in hells. That also is fun. This is the goal of philosophy: to know that I am the Infinite. Aims, motives, purposes, and duties live in the background. . . .

I am One, alone, through all eternity. Whom shall I fear? It is all my Self. This is continuously to be meditated upon. Through that comes realisation. It is through realisation that you become a blessing to others. . . . That is the goal.

If there is this truth, if there is God, it must be within us. I must be able to say, "I have seen Him with my eyes." Otherwise, I have no religion. Beliefs, doctrines, sermons do not make a religion. It is realisation, perception of God which alone is religion. . . .This world is real inasmuch as it contains a little bit of the reflection of that God. We love the good man because in his face shines the reflection a little more. We must catch it ourselves. There is no other way. That is the goal. Struggle for it!

From "Worshipper and Worshipped"

What we want is to see the man who is harmoniously developed—great in heart, great in mind, great in deed. We want the man whose heart feels intensely the miseries and sorrows of the world. And we want the man who not only can feel but can find the meaning of things, who delves deeply into the heart of nature and understanding. We want the man who will not even stop there, but who wants to work out the feeling and meaning by actual deeds. Such a combination of head, heart, and hand is what we want. There are many teachers in this world, but you will find that most of them are one-sided. One sees the glorious midday sun of intellect and sees nothing else. Another hears the beautiful music of love and can hear nothing else. Another is immersed in activity and has neither time to feel nor to think. Why not have the giant who is equally active, equally knowing, equally loving? Is it impossible? Certainly not. This is the man of the future, of whom there are only a few at present. The number of such will increase until the whole world is humanised.

I have been talking to you so long about intellect and reason. We have heard the whole of Vedanta. The veil of

Maya breaks; wintry clouds vanish, and the sunlight shines on us. I have been trying to climb the heights of the Himalayas, where the peaks disappear beyond the clouds. I propose to study with you the other side: the most beautiful valleys, the most marvelous exquisiteness in nature. . . .The glacier of the Himalayas must join hands with the rice fields of Kashmir. The thunderbolt must blend its base note with the warbling of birds. . . .

Is there any God? Is there anyone to be loved, any such one capable of being loved? Loving the stone would not be much good. We only love that which understands love, that which draws our love. So with worship. Never say that there is a man in this world of ours who worshipped a piece of stone as stone.

We find out that the omnipresent Being is in us. But how can we worship unless that being is separate from us? I can only worship Thee, and not me. I can only pray to Thee, and not to me. Is there any "Thou"?

The One becomes many. When we see the One, any limitations reflected through Maya disappear; but it is quite true that the manifold is not valueless. It is through the many that we reach the One.

Is there any Personal God—a God who thinks, who understands, a God who guides us? There is. The Impersonal God cannot have any one of these attributes. Each one of you is an individual: you think, you love, you hate, you are angry, sorry, and so on; yet you are impersonal, unlimited. You are personal and impersonal in one. You have the personal and the impersonal aspects. The impersonal reality cannot be angry, nor sorry, nor miserable—cannot even think misery. It cannot think, cannot know. It is knowledge itself. But the personal aspect knows, thinks, and dies, etc. Naturally, the universal Absolute must have two aspects: the one, the impersonal aspect, is the infinite reality of all things; the other, a personal aspect, is the Soul of our souls, Lord of all lords. It is He who creates this universe. Under His guidance this universe exists.

He, the Infinite, the Ever-Pure, the Ever-Free! He is no judge; God cannot be a judge. He does not sit upon a throne and judge between the good and the wicked. He is no magistrate, no general, no master. Infinitely merciful, infinitely loving is the Personal God.

Take it from another side. Every cell in your body has a soul conscious of the cell. It is a separate entity. It has a little will of its own, a little sphere of action of its own. All cells combined make up an individual. In the same way, the Personal God of the universe is made up of all these individuals.

Take it from still another side. You, as I see you, are as much of your absolute nature as has been limited and perceived by me. I have limited you in order to see you through the power of my eyes, my senses. As much of you as my eyes can see, I see. As much of you as my mind can grasp is what I know to be you, and nothing more. In the same way, I am reading the Absolute, the Impersonal, and see Him as Personal. As long as we have body and mind, we always see this triune being: God, nature, and soul. There must always be the three in one, inseparable. There is nature. There are human souls. There is again That in which nature and the human souls are contained.

The universal soul has become embodied. My soul itself is a part of God. He is the eye of our eyes, the life of our life, the mind of our mind, the soul of our soul. This is the highest ideal of the Personal God we can have.

If you are not a dualist but a monist, you can still have the Personal God. There is the One without a second. That One wanted to love Himself. Therefore, out of that One He made many. It is the big Me, the real Me, that the little me is worshipping. Thus in all systems you can have the Personal God.

From "Krishna"

This world is a play. You are His playmates. Go on and work, without any sorrow, without any misery! See His play in the slums, in the saloons!

Work to lift people! Not that they are vile or degraded, Krishna does not say that.

Do you know why so little good work is done? My lady goes to the slum. She gives a few ducats and says, "My poor man, take that and be happy." Or my fine woman, walking through the street, sees a poor fellow and throws him five cents. Think of the blasphemy of it! Blessed are we that the Lord has given us His teaching in your own Testament. Jesus says, "Inasmuch as ye have done it unto the least of these my brethren, ye have done it unto me." It is blasphemy to think that you can help anyone. First root out this idea of helping, and then go to worship. God's children are your Master's children. And children are but different forms of the father. You are His servant. Serve the living God. God comes to you in the blind, in the halt, in the poor, in the weak, in the diabolical. What a glorious chance for you to worship! The moment you think you are "helping," you undo the whole thing and degrade yourself. Knowing this, work. "What follows?" you say. You do not get that heartbreak, that awful misery. Work is no more slavery. It becomes a play and joy itself. Work! Be unattached! That is the whole secret. If you get attached, you become miserable.

With everything we do in life we identify ourselves. Here is a man who says harsh words to me. I feel anger coming on me. In a few seconds anger and I are one, and then comes misery. Attach yourselves to the Lord and to nothing else, because everything else is unreal. Attachment to the unreal will bring misery. There is only one Existence that is real, only one Life in which there is neither object nor subject.

But unattached love will not hurt you. Do anything— marry, have children. Do anything you like—nothing will hurt you. Do nothing with the idea of "mine." Duty for duty's sake; work for work's sake. What is that to you? You stand aside.

From "The Gita—III"

It is a tremendous error to feel helpless. Do not seek help from anyone. We are our own help. If we cannot help ourselves, there is none to help us. "Thou thyself art thine only friend, thou thyself thine only enemy. There is no other enemy but this self of mine, no other friend but myself." [Gita, 6.5] This is the last and greatest lesson, and oh, what a time it takes to learn it! We seem to get hold of it, and the next moment the old wave comes. The backbone breaks. We weaken and again grasp for that superstition and help. Just think of that huge mass of misery, and all caused by this false idea of going to seek for help! . . .

There is only one sin. That is weakness. When I was a boy I read Milton's *Paradise Lost*. The only good man I had any respect for was Satan. The saint is that soul that never weakens, faces everything, and determines to die game.

Stand up and die game! Do not add one lunacy to another. Do not add your weakness to the evil that is going to come. That is all I have to say to the world. Be strong! You talk of ghosts and devils. We are the living devils. The sign of life is strength and growth. The sign of death is weakness. Whatever is weak avoid! It is death. If it is strength, go down into hell and get hold of it! There is salvation only for the brave. "None but the brave deserves the fair." None but the bravest deserves salvation. Whose hell? Whose torture? Whose sin? Whose weakness? Whose death? Whose disease?

You believe in God. If you do, believe in the real God. "Thou art the man, Thou the woman, Thou the young man walking in the strength of youth, Thou the old man tottering with his stick." Thou art weakness, Thou art fear. Thou art heaven, and Thou art hell. Thou art the serpent that would sting. Come Thou as fear! Come Thou as death! Come Thou as misery!

All weakness, all bondage is imagination. Speak one word to it, it must vanish. Do not weaken! There is no other way out. Stand up and be strong! No fear. No superstition. Face the truth as it is! If death comes—that is the worst of our miseries—let it come! We are determined to die game. That is all the religion I know. I have not attained to it, but I am struggling to do it. I may not, but you may. Go on!

Where one sees another, one fears another. So long as there are two, there must be fear, and fear is the mother of all misery. Where none sees another, where it is all One, there is none to be miserable, none to be unhappy. [Adaption of *Chandogya Upanishad*, 7:23-24.] There is only the One without a second. Therefore be not afraid. Awake, arise, and stop not till the goal is reached!

The above extracts are from The Complete Works of Swami Vivekananda, *published by Advaita Ashrama, Calcutta.*